W.I.T.H. GOD

A 25-Day Devotional with God

CARLA R. CHALK

It's always a pleasure
to see your face daily.
You are beautiful inside
and out. May the grace of
God continue to carry. Keep
and bless you!
With love
Carla Chalk

Wisdom Identity Trust Healing

W.I.T.H. GOD

W.I.T.H. GOD: A 25-Day Devotional with God

Copyright © 2021 Carla R. Chalk

ISBN: 978-1-954595-11-8

Library of Congress Control Number: 2021919880

Sparkle Publishing
www.sparklepublishing.net

Printed in the USA.
Duncanville, Texas

Sparkle Publishing
Write. Publish. Sparkle.

DEDICATION

Thanking the Lord for this amazing opportunity and dedicating this devotional to my amazing children, Khayri and Emani, who sacrificed their time to let me complete this book.

To my great grandmother, Corene Creswell, in memoriam, who taught me at a young age that prayer is with God.

To my amazing friend, Rosyln Marks, who helped me birth the thought.

To my friend, Terry Dike, for being such an amazing man of God and a stellar individual.

To my sisters in Christ, Jordan Myles, Deonica Harris, and Jacqueline Rhone, for your amazing friendship, sisterhood, love, prayers, and presence in my life, which have always propelled me forward.

Table of Contents

Foreword by Terry Dike.. 1

Foreword by Dr. Timothy W. Sloan 3

Preface 5

Introduction 7

WISDOM 13

Day 1: Who God Created You to Be 14

Day 2: Don't Forget Who You Are 20

Day 3: Love 26

Day 4: Respect.. 30

Day 5: Respecting God.. 34

Day 6: Respecting Yourself 38

Day 7: Growing Discipleship 39

IDENTITY 45

Day 8: Everyone Has Their Own Route............................. 46

Day 9: Being Your Best You 48

Day 10: Don't Let Life Change Your Name...................... 53

Day 11: Don't Let Others Control Your Joy 57

Day 12: Don't Compare Yourself to Anyone 59

Day 13: Developing a Prayer Life...................................... 62

TRUST 70

    Day 14: Trusting God through the Good and Bad 68

    Day 15: Race to Him 75

    Day 16: Live for God, Not for People 79

    Day 17: Relationship with God 79

    Day 18: Learning How to Be Obedient 86

    Day 19: Persistence 90

    Day 20: When God Says No 90

    Day 21: Godly Community 97

HEALING 100

    Day 22: How to Deal with Your Heart 98

    Day 23: Forming Habits 104

    Day 24: Making Better Choices 108

    Day 25: Unforgiveness 112

Foreword
by Terry Dike

I applaud and celebrate anybody who has picked up this text to embark on downloading these gems of wisdom. This book is content-rich and packed with transparent examples of the author's journey to wholeness. This book brought me closer to Carla. Before your reading enjoyment, I wish to share more about Carla and my interactions with her over the last seven years. In those several years, I have seen the roller coaster, sometimes been on the roller coaster with her, now witnessing the triumphs. I have seen her parenting style. I have witnessed her laughs. On the flip side, I have sat with her at Chick-fil-A in North Houston as she cried. Like many women in this world, Carla carries so many responsibilities and, at times, in her mind, has lacked support. Her book will reveal the support she always had that she finally accepted.

I found myself thoroughly enjoying her analogies, teachings, and truth bombs. At times, I was shocked by her transparency. Carla's willingness to let down the veil and reveal her mistakes and the pain she experienced only increased my admiration of her struggle-victory testimony.

You may be a young person dealing with the pressures of teenage years, or you may be an adult reading along with your child or an adult with no children. Nevertheless, this book will help you, speak to you, and encourage you. Carla has traversed many fires and has made it through. You are hearing from an overcomer. She will not be lecturing to you or your child, rather sitting with you over a hot cup of tea and unpacking about the goodness of God.

"When you pray, God listens. When you listen, God talks, and when you believe, God works" (Carla).

Enjoy! I know I did.

Terry Dike

Foreword
by Dr. Timothy W. Sloan

I fondly remember as a young boy spending the afternoon at a local lake. Occasionally, some of our belonging would find their way into the water. Once it was too far to retain without going for a swim, we had to decide: Do we give up on our belongings and consider them lost, or do we find a way to retrieve them? We typically chose the latter.

Our strategy was simple. We would toss a rock in front of the item and allow the current to push it back. It wouldn't come speeding back to us in the blink of an eye, but the continuous current would ultimately return it.

Many of us often find ourselves in that same predicament and need a current to return to shore. I believe that's what Carla Chalk has done in this book. She created a devotional walk with God that acts as a current to draw us closer spiritually. And if we don't find ourselves adrift like a lost article, we can all use the work of a current to create more intimacy in our relationship with God.

I've had the privilege of being Carla's pastor and seeing up close her commitment to this journey. She does not write as a spectator, jeering those searching for closeness after being broken by life challenges. She writes with the reflection of her travels, willingly pulling back the curtains to her journey.

Carla has captured the road map in this devotional that we all need. This is not a copy-and-paste tool for your spiritual life. It is a resource to help you on your journey. It requires your attention and commitment.

So, wherever you find yourself, consider this your current for a closeness to God. Joining this journey will lead you to discover that God never gives up on what and who belongs to Him.

Dr. Timothy W. Sloan, Senior Pastor

The Luke Church

PREFACE

This book will guide you into **faith-shaping** conversations. It is my duty to offer Godly counsel to this nation by investing in God's people today. It is my prayer that through God's divine ability, all know how to deal with the journey that life brings and stand in faith. This is where reality and Biblical principles meet to change the world.

W.I.T.H God through:

Wisdom in making better choices,

Identity in who God created you to be,

Trusting God in all areas of your life,

Healing through God.

You can propel forward with faith
and the strength of God.

"God grant me the serenity, to accept the things I cannot change, the courage to change the things I can, and the wisdom to know the difference."

(Reinhold Niebuhr)

INTRODUCTION

In life we produce our own interpretation of who we think God created us to be. Sometimes, we make plans and believe that if we do this, this way, God will come and do what we want. But God is not a "this and that" kind of God with our plans. He is the God of all creation, and He knows all our needs. Before we were born, He planned our lives. In Jeremiah 1:5, God's Word says, "Before I formed you in the womb, I knew you. Before you were even born, I set you apart; I appointed you as a prophet to the nations."

So, before we were born, He had a plan for our lives. God **set us apart** and gave us a position. He knew who He created us to be so that we may willfully help His Kingdom. Of course, life happens, and we go through trials and tribulations, but through it all, He conditioned us to be **rooted and built up in Him (Colossians 2:7).**

I recall many adventures on my journey when I got lost along the way and forgot who God created me to be. I became disobedient and forgetful of God's Word. I began to try and do things on my own, in my own strength, and the way I thought it should be. In return, I picked up various lifestyles and bad habits, carried unforgiveness with me everywhere I went, and had no respect for myself, which squandered over into my relationships with friends and family. I had no joy or trust for anyone, including the Lord. This is never God's plan for our lives. He wants us to triumph in all areas of our lives and be wealthy, but we must follow His Word and decrees.

Psalm 1:1-3 says:

Blessed is the one who does not walk in step with the wicked or stand in the way that sinners take or sit in the company of mockers, but those whose delight is in the law of the Lord and meditates on his law, day and night. That person is like a tree planted by streams of water, which yields its fruit in season and whose leaf does not wither; whatever they do prospers.

I realized that I would never truly know who I am or who I was called to be without Him. I had to go back to God's Word and let go of the bad habits and harsh alternative lifestyles I was living. I no longer wanted to live the cycle of sin I was in, but because I didn't fully surrender it all to God, the same things festered in other areas of my life and relationships. It was a tough battle, but I began to put my trust back in God, giving Him my broken and scorned heart. Finally, I had to give it all to God completely. I had to **surrender completely**!

Proverbs 3:5-6 says, "Trust in the Lord with all your heart and lean not on your own understanding and in all your ways acknowledge Him so that he will direct your paths."

This Scripture gives clear direction:

If we:

1. Trust in Him with all your heart.

2. Lean not on your own understanding.

We cannot depend on our ability to understand everything God is doing, and we shouldn't try.

God will then:

3. Direct your paths.

What clearer direction do we need that will lead us into the paths He has laid out for us?

I completely understand how it feels to want to give up or believe God is not near. Unfortunately, in some cases, we do not know how to apply this Scripture to our lives, but I can give full testimony that if you do not know how to apply Proverbs 3:5-6 or any Scripture to your life, all you must do is open your heart and surrender to God and He will move on your behalf. God wants you to know who you are, but **He wants you to know yourself through Him.**

W.I.T.H. God, through wisdom, knowing your identity, trusting in Him, and continuously healing, you will walk in all the greatness that God created you to be. The surety is trusting God when life gets tough and learning to love God's people properly.

That will show your true character, and through a relationship with Him, you will grow.

He wants you to stand strong in His strength and never your own. So anytime you feel far from God, change your mindset and thank Him for being right next to you.

I want you to know that God is with you.

Do you want to know how I know?

Because **His Word never returns void**.

Deuteronomy 31:6 states, "Be strong and courageous. Do not fear or be in dread of them, for it is the Lord your God who goes with you. He will not leave you or forsake you."

His Word says that He will go with you and that He will never leave you or forsake you. This means He won't abandon you or give up on you. Even when you walk away, He is still with you. Open your heart to God and believe because all it takes is the size of a mustard seed of faith. Always remember that we walk by faith and not by sight (2 Corinthians 5:7). We can find ultimate fulfillment in a relationship with God. With man, this is impossible, but *W.I.T.H. God*, all things are possible (Matthew 19:26).

It is my prayer that this book will touch the depths of your heart and that the Word of God not only sticks to your mind but is written on the tablet of your heart. It is my prayer that you stand in the measure of faith that God has given you, and may you continuously draw from His living water when you feel depleted to know that God's Word is true and living and will carry you through life. We overcome by our testimony, so here's my devotion to you. May God bless you and keep you!

WISDOM

Day 1

Who God Created You to Be

Everyone has their own route, experiencing trials and tribulations, but our outcomes will not be the same. Each lesson will be received, handled, and learned differently. Similarly, every creation of God is unique.

Psalm 139: 13-16 states:

For you created my inmost being; you knit me together in my mother's womb. I praise you because I am fearfully and wonderfully made; your works are wonderful; I know that full well. My frame was not hidden from you when I was made in the secret place when I was woven together in the depths of the earth. Your eyes saw my unformed body; all the days ordained for me were written in your book before one of them came to be.

And Ephesians 2:10 reminds us, "For we are his creation, created in Christ Jesus for good works, which God prepared ahead of time so that we should walk in them."

God created you! You were created by a loving God, and you have great value. We may share likes and dislikes, find joy in the same hobbies, and even aspire to achieve the same goals in life, but the truth of the matter is God created you in His own image. You were created with a will, gifts, and divine purpose for your life. Some of us twist ourselves into knots trying to be something or someone else God did not design us to be. I used to observe other leaders, hoping to pray and help others overcome in the same way they did. In return, that made me hungry for someone else's purpose. I wanted to feel like I had done something and that God had given me a word that would set someone free. But my heart was not in the right place because I was reaching for someone else's calling when I had my own, which is **why it never works out when we are anything but ourselves**. It also can become an exhausting way to live, comparing ourselves to others when God has called us to be greater than we can even imagine. Deep inside of us, He has planted all we need, filling us with love, supernatural ability, exuberance, and tremendous value. We are valued in God's eyes, so why not love who God created you to be? You have your own name given to you at birth, and no matter who shares that name, it will always be called differently because **God calls all of us differently**!

You Are Called

Ephesians 4:4 states, "There is one body and one spirit, just as you were called to the one hope that belongs to your call."

God wants everyone to be saved under His love and guidance. And because we are called, **He calls us to salvation, sanctification, and service.**

Salvation

Ephesians 2:8-9 shares, "For you are saved by grace through faith, and this is not from yourselves, it is the gift of God. Not by works, so that no one can boast."

God declares us righteous for Jesus Christ:

"For He made Him who knew no sin to be sin for us, that we might become the righteousness of God in Him" (2 Corinthians 5:21).

If you would like to receive salvation, Romans 10: 9-10 states:

If you confess with your mouth the Lord Jesus and believe in your heart that God has raised Him from the dead, you will be saved. For with the heart, one believes unto righteousness, and with the mouth, confession is made unto salvation.

Read this prayer aloud:

Lord, I know I am a sinner, I repent, and I ask for your forgiveness for any word, deed, or thought I have committed that was unpleasing to you. I believe that you died for my sins and rose from the dead. Therefore, I turn from my sins and invite you to enter my life and heart. I want to trust you, follow you, and have my steps ordered by you as my Father, Lord, and Savior. In Jesus' name, Amen.

If you read this prayer out loud, it means that your sins have been forgiven. Salvation separates you from sin. It does not mean that your life will be free from sin, but that you have a choice to turn from your wicked ways. You are making healthy and conscious decisions because you are called differently. It's a daily commitment!

Sanctification

God sets us apart for His purposes.

Romans 12:2 reminds us, "Do not be conformed to the pattern of this world but be transformed by the renewing of the mind."

Through sanctification, we are free from sin and purified. Sanctification does not mean we will have a perfect life, but through obedience and commitment, there will be a continuous change by God, freeing us from sinful habits. We then take on the characteristics of Jesus. **His fruit of the Spirit is love, joy, peace, patience, kindness, goodness, faithfulness, gentleness, and**

self-control (Galatians 5:22-23). Our actions show the fruit we bear. As we walk with God, people will see the God in us by how we carry ourselves and treat others. Sanctification is growth.

Service

"As for me and my house, we will serve the Lord" (Joshua 24:15).

Service means that we were given life to contribute to the Kingdom. Our job is to serve Him by accomplishing what God has planned for us. You have been chosen to carry out His work in the world. We were designed to make a difference. As we make a difference, God supplies us with what we need, fastening us together with Him. And because God is love, a requirement for us is to love all His people. We owe no one anything in this world but to love them. As we serve God by loving Him, His outpour through us will help us love others and teach us how to serve in His Kingdom.

Reflection

Through sanctification, we are purified.

Do you believe salvation separates you from sin? If so, how will you conduct yourself?

_____

_____

_____

_____

What fruit of the Spirit do you embody today or want to improve?

_____

_____

_____

_____

What does service mean to you?

_____

_____

_____

_____

DAY 2

DON'T FORGET WHO YOU ARE

There are moments in life when we forget who we are. Sometimes, we get lost in the ways of this world, which causes us to think less of ourselves. In those moments, it is easy to forget how strong you were before trouble hit, how you already overcame your past, and how you are no longer who you used to be. It's easy to go back into old habits because new ways look frightening. But **God makes us strong for the journey,** and **it is because of His power that we are who we are today.**

As I journeyed through life, there were many times I forgot who I was. I felt lost and confused. Sometimes, I was mentally and physically lost because I felt like I had no direction, and the leaders that I stepped to for help listened to my needs but turned me away with "get closer to God, and then I'll help you," or they just listened to be nosy, to say they knew something about me. As a result, I felt depleted. Depression stayed knocking at my door. The enemy wanted my mind and would do anything to ensure that my mind was focused on all the negative things in my life. Occasionally, suicide would knock at my door, patiently waiting for me to answer. I will admit that I opened that door feeling fear, but as you can see, I am writing to you. The enemy would tell me that my problems were bigger than God, but I soon realized that God was bigger than any problem I could ever face.

God said it was not my time and wanted to show me who I was in Him. Notice how I used the word "feeling." When it comes to God, we cannot rely on our emotions. **We must stand in full faith. We must stand knowing who we are**. Because I didn't know who I was, that gave room for the enemy to tell me who I was and that I was less than who God called me to be. Whatever room you give the enemy, he will step in and move fast to gain control over the authority God has given you. He will attempt to hinder you with distractions from every direction. Because God has given you the authority to trample over the enemy's head (Luke 10:19), **the enemy has no say-so over who you are**.

Did you know that who you are sets you apart from everyone else in the world, that your testimony only belongs to you and could change the world when you are ready to tell it? Did you know that your uniqueness solely belongs to you? There are gifts inside of you, placed by God, that make you who you are. If you tie your testimony and the gifts of God together, your voice and faith could change a nation. When you stand strong on who you are, you will be able to stand against the enemy with power. If you don't know who you are, seek God and ask Him to tell you. He would love to tell you who you are so that no one else can put a label on you. Stand strong on who God says you are.

Here are a few scriptures of who God says you are:

1. I am a child of God (John 1:12).

2. God loves me and has chosen me (1 Thessalonians 1:4).

3. I have been accepted by Christ (Romans 15:7).

4. The peace of God guards my heart and mind (Philippians 4:7).

5. I am God's workmanship created to produce good works (Ephesians 2:10).

6. In Christ, I have wisdom, righteousness, sanctification, and redemption (1 Corinthians 1:30).

Know that God has chosen you because He loves you! **Your yes to who God says you are matters**. What you speak out about yourself should be affirmations of inspiration. What you tell yourself daily matters. You must cover yourself and your thoughts daily because the enemy will try and wiggle in any space you allow to change your mind. Covering yourself means asking God to cover you in His full armor.

Ephesians 6:13-18 states:

Therefore, put on the full armor of God so that when the day of evil comes, you may be able to stand your ground, and after you have done everything, to stand. Stand firm then, with **the belt of truth** buckled around your waist, with **the breastplate of righteousness** in place, and with your **feet fitted with the readiness that comes from the gospel of peace**. In addition to all this, take up **the shield of faith**, with which you can extinguish all the flaming arrows of the evil one. Take **the helmet of salvation** and **the sword of the Spirit**, which is the word of God. And pray in the Spirit on all occasions with all kinds of prayers and requests. With this in mind, be alert and always keep on praying for all the Lord's people.

The enemy will tell you that you are the opposite of what God's Word says. **Anything that contradicts God's Word, throw it right out!** When the enemy tries to instill fear, stand on faith because you have the authority to tell the enemy: **"God has not given me the spirit of fear, but of power and of love and a sound mind"** (2 Timothy 1:7).

Stick to God's Word because His Word will never steer you in the wrong direction. Do not let others tell you who you are; always ask God. So, keep all these things in mind the next time you wonder about yourself.

I am bold. I am loved. I am fearfully and wonderfully made. I am the head and not the tail.

You have everything you need inside of you!

Reflection

Use this area to rewrite those affirmations for the next five days.

Day 1

_____

_____

_____

_____

_____

Day 2

_____

_____

_____

_____

_____

Day 3

_____

_____

_____

_____

_____

Day 4

_____

_____

_____

_____

_____

Day 5

_____

_____

_____

_____

_____

DAY 3

LOVE

We've all heard the expression "love is blind," but how does that expression apply to you? Does it fall under being in relationships that you are blinded by what you think is love, so you fall for anything, or have you failed to realize that God loves you no matter what and that **there is nothing you can do that God can't love you out of**?

Sometimes, we can be so wound up in this world that we cannot receive the love of God or receive love from the people He has placed in our lives. In 1 Corinthians 13:4-7, God gives us a list of things that tells us what defines love. Indeed, we've had our share of what we think love is based on how it was given to us growing up, our expectations of love from others, and our value of love in friendships and romantic relationships. We can even consider the way we love ourselves, which is particularly important.

I grew up not knowing what love is because it was not shown to me. I was not raised on I love yous and hugs of comfort. Love was shown to me in all the relationships I was in while living to survive. But I learned that if we allow the love of God to fill us, our outpour will resemble what He asks us to show ourselves and others.

Let us look at what 1 Corinthians 13:4-7 says so we can put it in our hearts:

Love is patient. Love is kind. It does not envy. It does not boast. It is not proud. It does not dishonor others. It is not self-seeking, it is not easily angered, it keeps no record of wrongs. Love does not delight in evil but rejoices with the truth. It always protects, always trusts, always hopes, always perseveres.

God calls us to love. He calls us to love ourselves because He loves us. He calls us to love our neighbor as we love ourselves. He calls us to love because love conquerors all. Love is the greatest and first commandment. **Love always protects.** It watches out for others. When we or our loved ones fall short, love will cover us. The type of love that God gives us exceeds the love we could ever receive from anyone else. **Love always trusts**, and because of love, it allows us to trust God and others. Trust allows us to believe in the things of God and leads us to stand strong, knowing that when our focus is on the Lord, His love will overpower every situation. **Love always hopes**, and with hope in Jesus Christ, we have faith in who He is in our lives. Because He lives in us, He will shine through us. With the love we show other individuals, we can give them hope. Our positive actions make a positive impact on the lives of others. Where they once felt inadequate will give them hope and love for the future. **Love**

always perseveres. It endures all things. Because **God's love is everlasting, it is rooted in the heart**.

What is your definition of love?

Is it an intense feeling of deep affection?

Love is not an emotion. It is an action.

Love shows in the way we treat ourselves and others.

Is your love patient and kind?

Does your love let you love others that may have wronged you?

Love is forgiveness, compassion, unconditional, and without judgment. But let's be honest. Human nature can get in the way of how we love, causing us to hold back, meaning we love but cannot love as God calls us. As we surrender our hearts and lives to Jesus, He will abide in us, and His love through us will touch others: "Beloved, let us love one another, for love is from God, and whoever loves has been born of God and knows God. Anyone who does not love does not know God, because God is love" (1 John 4:7-8).

Loving God above all else is when we are at our happiest. **No one can make us happy and fill us with love like God**. Therefore, we must declutter our envious and self-seeking ways and boastful thoughts because we are not better than the next person, no matter the achievements in life. Let the love of

God guide you into the right relationships. Create the space for Him to dwell inside you and continuously show you true love.

Reflection

What are your thoughts about love?

_____

_____

_____

_____

_____

_____

_____

_____

How has love treated you?

_____

_____

_____

_____

_____

_____

_____

_____

Day 4

Respect

These days, respect is hard to come by. Some people have no respect for the value of life. Because respect is taught, many do not know how to properly respect others or show people how to treat them because it was never taught. It won't just come naturally in a world full of chaos, anger, lies, and deceit. The burden is heavy because people are lost mentally, physically, and spiritually. The world has lost respect for the things of God and His people. We no longer accept and love people for who they are. Instead, we judge people on the things they have, how they dress, the house they live in, and the car they drive. We idolize people because of their fame, and a desire develops for what they have. But does that really matter? Aren't all those things just materialistic that can be gone instantly? If God were to take everything you had today, all you would have is you and God. Would that not be enough for you? What does respect mean to you?

How would you respect yourself and the people around you if you truly knew what it meant to respect the things of life with God?

Respect is a deep admiration for someone, or something caused by their qualities or talents.

If we only respect people because of their abilities, qualities, and achievements, are we really respecting them? In reality, we are only respecting parts about them. Respect builds trust and safety. Respect means working on your vertical relationship *(you and God)* and treating Him with the utmost respect He deserves to learn how to respect our horizontal relationships, which is *fellowship* through Him. Notice how I mentioned "through Him." Through Him, we can possess those qualities that show us how to continuously remain in a place to honor and respect God and everyone we encounter. Let God lead and show you how to respect Him, yourself, and others. **Respect is knowing that you matter and are valued.**

Reflection

How do you value yourself?

_____

_____

_____

_____

_____

_____

_____

_____

What does respect and value look like to you?

_____

_____

_____

_____

_____

_____

_____

_____

_____

DAY 5

RESPECTING GOD

The most important thing a person can do is respect God and obey His commands because He knows everything we do, even our innermost secrets. He knows about all the good and bad, and **He is the only one that can judge us for what we do.**

Respecting God means obeying Him. If we love God with our heart, soul, and mind (Matthew 22: 37-38), we move out of our way and regard Him with honor. This means putting God first in all things and thinking of Him before making decisions. It means that we respect everything He stands for, His creations of this world, and everything He has blessed us with, including our love for His people. We should **take nothing for granted**. Respecting Him means you admire Him and find value in the life He has blessed you to live. When we respect God, we fulfill our responsibilities to Him. In return, He will bless our lives abundantly because His desire is for all of us to live a life in overflow, a wealthy life full of His riches and glory: "May every one of you overflow with the grace and favor of our Lord Jesus Christ" (Philippians 4:23 PT).

There is no greater feeling than knowing you are pleasing God and that you have a true relationship with Him.

Respecting God means honoring Him for giving you another day. If you were given another day, that means you still have a purpose on this Earth. Therefore, **you must make time for the things of God**. Instead of setting your alarm to get up for work or school, set it a few minutes early to spend time with God and reference Him properly. Sometimes, we wake up and begin our day thinking that telling God good morning is enough. I'm here to tell you that it's not enough. You must go deeper.

Did you know you can talk to God, just like you talk to someone on the phone? God loves conversation. You can tell Him about your day and when you're hurt, angry, happy, and sad. You can even tell Him when you're mad at Him. And guess what? He will understand! He would rather hear from you than not hear from you at all. I used to get up and not think twice about God. I moved as I pleased, doing whatever I wanted and with whoever I wanted. God saved me from so much, and I didn't think to give Him thanks. But because it was not taught to me, I did not know how to reference God. I did not know to give God thanks in all things. I did not know that I was still alive because of Him and that He protects us from things that we don't even know about. That's called seen and unseen danger. I had clothes on my back and a roof over my head, all because of Him. **He is our provider**. God kept me, and I didn't know it was Him that did it all! Worship Him today for all He has done!

Respect is worshiping God and God only. He deserves our worship.

Reflection

Today, dig deeper into what you can change in your life to make sure you fully respect God and the things He asks of you.

Ask for His guidance, and He will lead you.

How will you now honor and respect God?

_____

_____

_____

_____

_____

_____

_____

_____

_____

_____

_____

_____

_____

_____

Day 6

Respecting Yourself

We just discussed respecting God. Well, a part of respecting God is respecting yourself. Self-respect is protecting your space and the things you value. It is letting go of people, places, and things that no longer serve you. I remember when I did not respect God or myself. I did not reference Him for anything in my life. I was led by my self-seeking thoughts and made no time to find value in myself. I had a broken spirit, low self-esteem, and fake confidence. My confidence was based on material things and the abilities that I could provide for others. But those things never carried any weight. It seemed to always bring me right back down with no respect for myself. I slept with whoever I wanted, club hopped because I could, and hung out in the streets late at night with no purpose.

I did not respect myself. When you respect yourself, you love yourself and every flaw. No one will be able to tell you that you look good or feed you fake love to talk you out of your pants. You won't have to go on dates to get a free meal, and you won't have to spend your time dating multiple people to fill voids. **When you respect yourself, you are satisfied with yourself and fulfilled with what God has invested in you**. God wants you to be able to look in the mirror and see yourself the way He sees you. Having respect for yourself will help you to evaluate your values. No one will be able to come in and deter you in the opposite direction of where the Lord is trying to take you. You will no longer be driven by the material things of this world.

Romans 12:2 states:

Do not be conformed to this world, but be transformed by the renewal of your mind, that you may discern what is good and acceptable and perfect, will of God.

As you respect yourself, you honor God. The things of the world will not capture you or be able to hold you in bondage. You will be able to discern the Will of God, knowing what is good and acceptable. The renewal of your mind is a daily process. It is a constant practice of building positive thoughts and throwing out the negative as soon as it enters. Ask God to renew your mind, ensuring that your thoughts remain pure and always align with Him.

Reflection

What or who are you willing to let go of in your life that no longer serves you or helps you to grow?

_____

_____

_____

_____

_____

_____

What changes do you need to make to respect yourself?

_____

_____

_____

_____

_____

_____

"Respect yourself enough to walk away from anything that no longer serves you, grows you, or makes you happy."

(Robert Tew)

Day 7

Growing Discipleship

As we grow, we undergo development that is natural but purely for the spirit in us. This type of growth does not mean increasing size or physical change but growing mentally and spiritually – *mentally* growing into our Father and *spiritually* growing into grace.

"Instead, speaking the truth in love, we are to grow to become in every respect the mature body of him who is the head, that is, Christ" (Ephesians 4:15). "But grow in the grace and knowledge of our Lord and Savior Jesus Christ. To him be glory both now and forever! Amen" (2 Peter 3:18).

As we grow in grace, we are not obtaining more grace but maturing as Christians. We are to grow in the grace and knowledge of God to have an intimate relationship with Him. As we grow in discipleship with obedience, our character transforms to be more like Him. **God has called people to represent Him on Earth, people like us!** As we grow in discipleship, we build courage, become consistent, and change. **You will make all the difference in this world when you know yourself**. Discipleship allows us to speak the truth lovingly, giving sound doctrine to those tailored to our journey. The more we grow into Him, the more others will see Him in us. Growing discipleship means that I am putting God's truth into action, I am a believer and follower of Christ, and that my life models His Word.

Reflection

What in your life models Jesus?

_____

_____

_____

_____

_____

_____

_____

_____

How would you like to change the world?

_____

_____

_____

_____

_____

_____

_____

_____

IDENTITY

Day 8

Everyone Has Their Own Route

At birth, we are born with a mark on our bodies. This mark is a birthmark. A birthmark is an unusual, typically permanent brown or red mark that separates us from each other because no mark is the same. This birthmark comes in all shapes and sizes, just like us, and adds to our identity.

Genesis 1:27 states, "So God created man in His own image, in the image of God he created Him; male and female He created them."

God designed you in His own way, and you have a uniqueness about you that no one else can take. God does everything with purpose, including intentionally creating you. So, no matter what you've been through, making it through the storm has a purpose for your growth.

That may seem crazy because you might look at your circumstances and wonder how they could be intentional.

What if I was adopted?

What if I grew up without my parents?

What if I was molested?

What if drugs or alcohol have been a part of my family?

I can agree that life's situations can be harsh, but if you're reading this today, I am here to tell you that you are a survivor. If you weren't a survivor, this book would not be in your hands. All circumstances were purposed for growth and for you to be used by God to help someone else. **Anything in life that you've overcome, you now have the authority to help the next individual overcome as well**.

But the course and quality of your life will be determined by how you handle what you didn't see coming. God knows the plan He has for you. It says it in His Word: "For I know the plans that I have for you, declares the Lord, plans to prosper you and not to harm you, plans to give you hope and a future" (Jeremiah 29:11).

His plans are His preferences, what He sees for you, which requires your participation.

What do I mean by participation?

I'm referring to obedience, participating by doing the right thing at every opportunity. In those choices, God will lead you down the right path. Everyone has their own route, but it's up to you to take the right path and be a leader. God wanting it for you is not enough. You must want it! The world is your mission field. **You have been given an identity with power and authority**.

Do not remain comfortable in someone else's identity. Stay your route but keep God first!

Reflection

Where do you think you are headed in life?

_____

_____

_____

_____

_____

_____

_____

_____

What route (steps) are you taking to stay focused?

_____

_____

_____

_____

_____

_____

_____

_____

Day 9

Being Your Best You

We often hear the following sentiments:

Always do your best!

Give it your all!

But what about being your best you?

No one can replace you or beat you at being you. Being your best means you are in control of your feelings, letting no one steal your joy, and that you no longer blame anyone for your actions or where you are in life. Being your best means that you protect your space and find value in who you are, no matter who that separates you from in life.

I am at my best when taking every opportunity to make better choices and when I put 100% effort to look beyond negativity and pursue the things of God with eagerness. I remember when I used to work out with a trainer, and he would give me an exercise to do, which meant I was usually counting out to 25. When my trainer wasn't around, I would skip count. When he would come back, I'd say I had done the work. I lied, and the only person I was hurting was myself. I was shorting myself of the work I needed to better myself. I didn't make any progress because I wanted to take shortcuts. I didn't put in the work to achieve my goal. Isn't this the same way we treat life sometimes?

2 Timothy 2:15 reminds us: "Do your best to present yourself to God as one approved, a worker who does not need to be ashamed and who correctly handles the word of truth."

We short ourselves of our potential by taking shortcuts and not believing in ourselves or procrastinating when we know we have work to do. But guess what? When I began to do the work that my trainer asked of me, I found out how strong I was and didn't have to cheat myself. I became stronger and stronger. I began to believe in myself. Some days, I was very tired and wanted to quit, but I pressed on. I felt good, but mentally, I was even stronger. Let's add God to this scenario.

God = the Trainer

God wants to train us to build us up and strengthen the spirit within. When we don't obey what He asks, we short ourselves of who He created us to be. We won't know how powerful we are if we don't do our best to be all that God has called us to be. Do your part, and God can and will move in mighty ways to continuously help you excel in life. To be your best you, you must **ask God for less of you and more of Him**.

Reflection

What are you willing to surrender to be your best you?

_____

_____

_____

_____

_____

_____

_____

_____

What does being your best you look like?

_____

_____

_____

_____

_____

_____

_____

_____

Day 10

Don't Let Life Change Your Name

Life can be challenging. Sometimes, because of our circumstances, we let life change us. It's all about perspective, how you look at your situations and how you handle them. Don't let your situations handle you. There are some things in life that we have no control over and cannot change. In those moments, it's best to **surrender to God because when we hold onto things, it only hinders us** from learning what was meant for us to grow.

Are you learning from your mistakes, or have you become a repeat offender of a vicious cycle?

Cycles will have you doubting yourself. Cycles will tell you that you are never getting out, that you will never change, and that you will never be anything. Cycles can have you doubting yourself when you are breaking free, or they can send you right back into bondage through your thoughts. But it's all a lie from the pit of hell. You must stand firm. **"A double-minded man is unstable in all his ways" (James 1:8).**

You must know that no matter what life throws at you, you will get back up and try again and that God is by your side. Did you know that **failure only occurs when you stay down**? When we let the failures of life defeat us, we begin to change our name. And God hasn't changed your name. I'm not talking about the name our parents gave us, but the name God has given us. **We are conquerors, blessed, called, loved, valued, and anointed**. We are overcomers. Although it may not seem like it, you have already survived your situation, even if you are still in it. **You are a survivor!** But do you believe that you are an overcomer?

I have overcome so much in life but didn't know because of my perspective. I was so stuck on the things that were done to me or who I wanted to be that I could not see the victory in my triumph. I was just out here existing instead of living. I wasn't living out who I was called to be. Because we live in a fragmented world where everything calls us toward greediness, selfishness, and despair, we must not let the world and our circumstances change our name. Our poor choices steal our joy, falter our plans, kill our dreams, and diminish our perspectives, but God gives us strength, hope, joy, and perseverance to push through. And because you were fearfully and wonderfully made by the hands of Jesus, we must keep our God-given name. When we doubt ourselves, condemnation can creep in like a thief in the night. But there is no condemnation for those who are in Christ Jesus (Romans 8:1), so focus on Him and always remember where your roots stand. They stem from the Lord. His Word says that we are rooted and built up in Him (Colossians 2:7).

Just in case you need a reminder of your roots, here are some Bible scriptures to keep with you:

Strength: Psalm 46:1

Hope: Romans 15:4

Joy: Psalm 126: 2-3

Perseverance: Romans 5:3-4

Reflection

What does your name mean to you?

_____

_____

_____

_____

_____

_____

_____

_____

Make a list of what makes you, you (and stand on who you are).

_____

_____

_____

_____

_____

_____

_____

_____

_____

DAY 11

DON'T LET OTHERS CONTROL YOUR JOY

Often, we put our joy in the hands of others, yet joy should be something that others can't control. I say this because **joy is our responsibility. Joy is in the heart and of the soul. It is a practice and behavior**. It's a choice that is purposely made. If we've made joy a feeling based on how others make us feel, then we have lost focus on its meaning.

I remember times when I was in relationships, and my happiness was predicated on that individual. I would wake up, and they would be the first thing on my mind and the last thing on my mind before going to bed. So, if I didn't talk to them when I got up or before I went to bed, my days were thrown off, and my nights were restless. But where was God in the equation? If they were the first thing on my mind in the morning, that means I hadn't prayed and made time for God because my focus was elsewhere. And if they were the last thing on my mind before bed, I had not thought to pray with God before bed. I spent my nights on the phone with that individual until I fell asleep, or I was up wondering why they hadn't called me yet. This pattern left room for the enemy to help keep my focus on the wrong things due to the door I opened. I was focused on the wrong relationship and allowed those moments to lead my days. If I were focused on my relationship with God, my mornings would be full of joy, no matter who talks to me. We can't control what others do, so that makes us responsible for maintaining our peace.

If we investigate what joy means Biblically, we learn that **joy is a spirit** (Galatians 5: 22-23): **"But the fruit of the Spirit is love, joy, peace, forbearance, kindness, goodness, faithfulness, gentleness, and self-control.** Against such things, there is no law."

God gives us joy because He lives in us. **Joy brings meaning to life**. Sometimes, we look for joy in all the wrong places, and that's because there is a difference between joy and happiness. Happiness is an external expression, while joy is internal. Joy couples with meaning and purpose and is maintained no matter the trials and tribulations. The joy of the Holy Spirit will help you bring encouragement instead of drama, teach you how to naturally and unconditionally show love toward others. We all need the Holy Spirit, and what better way to live than with the fruit of the Spirit dwelling within. Notice I said the fruit of the Spirit and not spirits because they are packed in one. We are to house the fruit of the Spirit, and because He lives in you, others will be able to see the fruit you bear by your actions. God does not call you what other people call you. He calls you what He created you to be.

Filling you with pure love, peace, and joy would be His pleasure, so tap in!

Reflection

What brings meaning to your life?

_____

_____

_____

_____

_____

_____

_____

_____

How will you maintain your joy?

_____

_____

_____

_____

_____

_____

_____

_____

Day 12

Don't Compare Yourself to Anyone

It's often easy to get caught up in what we see others doing. And sometimes we can be plain nosey, always minding the business of others instead of our own. We see them doing remarkable things with their lives or making poor choices. In some cases, when we see individuals doing momentous things in their life, we want the same if we are not there yet. We begin to want what they have or try to achieve the same, not knowing what or how long it took them to achieve such accomplishments. I'm sure we are all aware that nothing happens overnight, not even when we wish upon a star.

Galatians 6:4-5 reminds us:

Pay careful attention to your own work, for then you will get the satisfaction of a job well done, and you won't need to compare yourself to anyone else, for we are each responsible for our own conduct.

The good thing is that anything is possible because of the Father we serve, but what God has for you is for you, and what they've achieved is for them. God has placed unique gifts within you and wants you to be able to use them. He wants us to live in overflow, with abundance in every area of our lives. Let God control your life because you won't be able to accomplish the plans He has for you by looking at others. When you try to obtain the same goals as someone else and walk their path, it does not turn out the way you expected because it's not your journey to travel. I remember when I would scroll on social media and see so many people going exactly where I was headed. In those moments, I talked down about myself because I wasn't there yet. I began to tell myself that I needed to do more and convinced myself that I was behind, which can cause you to rush when things are really done in God's timing. The true statement was, I was right where God needed me to be because I knew I had been obedient. It's okay to let others be an inspiration, but never compare yourself; instead, use that inspiration to push yourself to reach your goals. Be intentional about being intentional. Be your best you and be great at it!

Reflection

What areas in your life can you be more intentional about?

_____

_____

_____

_____

_____

_____

_____

What is conducive to your growth?

_____

_____

_____

_____

_____

_____

_____

_____

DAY 13

DEVELOPING A PRAYER LIFE

Prayer is our greatest communication with God that should be implemented daily. Taking the time to say thank you, Lord, for another day before your feet hit the floor. Today, you woke up in your right mind with a pumping heart and an opportunity to rejoice before the Lord. We often forget that yesterday could have been our last day on Earth and that someone else did not wake up today, yet you were given another day. Instead, we roll over, grab our cell phones, scroll through social media, and check for missed calls and emails before we thank God. In our busy schedules, we forget to pray and give thanks, and yet the whole day has gone by, and you realize you haven't spoken or prayed with God, or you probably haven't recognized it at all.

But who is perfect?

No one!

I've been there before. I had to create a habit of prayer, meaning getting up 30 minutes to an hour earlier to read the Word and spend time with God. This meant putting God first and giving Him my time at the start of my day so that He could lead my day. I made a conscious decision that I would not do anything until I had communicated with Him first, sometimes just sitting in silence and welcoming Him in my presence before I start my day or taking His hand and walking through the day together. Prayer is seeking God with all your heart. **When you pray, God listens; when you listen, God talks, and when you believe, God works**. "Rejoice always, pray without ceasing, give thanks in all circumstances; for this is the will of God in Christ Jesus for you" (1 Thessalonians 5:16-18).

Seeking God with all your heart will strengthen your prayer life. It will give you a continuous hunger as you pray out to Him, which will grow you in unimaginable ways. Praying without ceasing means praying while walking, driving, working, hanging out, laying down, and at any moment, big or small. This does not have to be done out loud. You can pray in your mind and heart, and the Father will hear you. Communication with God goes a long way. We're not just communicating with God for things of monetary value but an increase in faith, protection, spiritual growth, family, and friends. In all those things, even in our lowest moments, give thanks because **it's in our prayers that our greatest barriers are overcome**, and He will keep and see you through it all. His Word says that this is the Will of God in Christ Jesus for you. **This prayer life is for you!** Developing a prayer life is an opportunity to spend time with God, and the only way to understand God's heart is through prayer. **Consistent prayer releases the power of God's blessing in your life** and circumstances, giving us access to God's power and purpose.

Today, I ask you to find the value in prayer and enjoy the presence of the Holy Spirit.

"Prayer is, at root, simply paying attention to God."

(Dr. Ralph Martin)

Reflection

If you haven't already, how will you incorporate prayer in your life?

_____

_____

_____

_____

_____

_____

_____

Ask God to increase your prayer life, and be prepared to be consistent.

_____

_____

_____

_____

_____

_____

_____

TRUST

Day 14

Trusting God through the Good and Bad

The act and word "trust" were always tough for me. Growing up, I didn't trust many people, which carried into my adulthood. I hid behind the statements "I'm a private person," "I don't want anyone in my business," and "I don't want people to see me cry." Instead, I held everything in. I always thought people would turn on me, so there was no point in getting close. That seeped over into me not fully trusting God, if at all. I held in as much as I could, never giving Him my hurt, anger, and depression because I felt like I couldn't receive healing in those areas. I leaned on no one, including God. Sometimes, I was ashamed, and because I didn't trust God, I thought He wouldn't do anything. So, I remained stagnant. But was He not going to heal me in those areas, or was I just so shut off that I didn't let Him in to intervene on my behalf?

We know to thank Him and show great excitement because He came through in a time of need, but how do we reference God on the down days? You know, those days when you get up and feel like you are going to have a crappy day, had a restless night, feel upset with someone for not sticking to their word, were stabbed in the back by someone you thought was a friend, or feel upset with God because He didn't move when you wanted Him to move?

How do you handle those situations?

Who do you lean on when times get tough?

It's okay to call on your friends, but it is very important to know **God is the main source and your friends are the resource.** Consult with God first, and then you can call a friend. We can't put God in a box, thinking He will only come through for the material things. In fact, He wants to deal with everything pertaining to you. It's easy to put up a wall and hold on to hurt, anger, and depression. However, that will leave room for you to wallow in defeat. But **we are not defeated people because the battle has already been won**. Surrendering it all to God and trusting Him to deal with your pain and problems are key! I've experienced several moments in life when I didn't know how to deal with my heart. I let so many unhealthy things fester in my heart. One day, I gave it all to God because I no longer wanted to hang onto the pain. I wanted to trust Him because He could take it all away and fill me with love, peace, and joy.

So, how do you give it to God?

Well, when we give it all to God, that means **we cannot pray and worry**. It means that once we ask God to handle the situation, we do our best not to let it hinder our hearts or let our actions become negative. We must believe in the things we pray to God. It means standing in full faith that God will come through for us. And because we only need faith the size of a mustard seed, God can and will do remarkable things. When we give it all to God, we shouldn't attempt to take matters into our own hands. It's all about learning to trust God through whatever season you're in, good or bad. This also means that once you give it to God, don't look or go backward. When you feel like He's not moving fast enough or the way you want, you try and take matters into your own hands, and it brings you right back to worrying. Sometimes, we must get out of our own way so that God can move in our lives the way He pleases. Let God lead you. **We want His Will, not our will to be done.**

Reflection

What will you surrender to God so that you can trust Him fully?

_____

_____

_____

_____

Make sure you do not pick up the things you've surrendered to God.

_____

_____

_____

_____

Remember: You can't pray and worry. Whatever you ask of God, stand in the belief of what you are praying for and that you are more than capable to receive if it's in His Will for your life.

_____

_____

_____

_____

Day 15

Race to Him

In a race, all the runners run, but only one gets the prize. Typically, individuals who compete in games go into strict training. They train to strengthen themselves and win. In that process, they do what it takes to remain healthy, prepared, and ready to win.

Have you ever competed in a game or activity you enjoy? You're doing your best in those moments because you love the activity or are competitive and want to win. When we want to win, we do our best to ensure we play our best and work hard to come out ahead.

So, let's apply this to our daily lives!

1 Corinthians 9:24-26 states:

Do you not know that in a race all the runners run, but only one gets the prize? Run in such a way as to get the prize. Everyone who competes in the games goes into strict training. They do it to get a crown that will not last, but we do it to get a crown that will last forever. Therefore, I do not run like someone running aimlessly; I do not fight like a boxer beating the air.

What does your life look like when you are not competing in an activity? In competition, we give our all to the things of importance to us, but what about the things that are important to God? Do you give your all when it comes to spending time with God or doing the things He asks of you? Let's be honest. **If you do things in laziness, your results will return the same**. What you put out is what you get! Look at it this way – the real race is our effort with God. He wants more effort than we put into our games, goals, and objectives. He wants us to chase after Him. He wants our time and best efforts to study His Word, spending time with Him, and getting to know and understand Him. A simple conversation with Him goes a long way. He always wants to hear your voice, no matter the topic.

In sporting races, the competition is for that number one spot. In our effort with our Creator, there is no competition; His prize will last forever, which is eternal life. But we must make Him number one in our minds, lives, and hearts. In your relationship with Christ, we don't have to compete to be number one because He already lives inside of us. The reality of life is that God does not want to be put second, just as you would not want to be second in any relationship. When you've prepared for something, you come with full confidence and faith that you're going to win. To prepare for a race, you must practice building your strength. The more you practice, the stronger you become. The same applies to our Savior. The more you seek Him, the more you can see your true strength and capabilities through Him. In your prayer life, you must seek Him with humility and seek Him by surrendering. You must put your foot down at the mark and begin the race when God says go, and you must give it your all!

Reflection

Remember, what you put out is what you get in return. What you sow, you will reap. Share an honest assessment of what you've been sowing into your relationship with God.

_____

_____

_____

_____

_____

_____

Sow in studying and spending time in His Word and getting to know Him.

_____

_____

_____

_____

_____

_____

THE FATHER LOVES YOU!

Day 16

Live for God, Not for People

Everyone was born into this world with a purpose. That purpose is to live for God and not for people. Ephesians 2:10 states, "For we are his workmanship created in Christ Jesus unto good works which God hath before ordained that we should walk in them."

That verse tells us that we are Christ's creation, created for Him to do His good works and we are already prepared because it was ordained, which means we are to be led by God, pleasing Him and not family and friends. He is our focus! Sometimes, we get so caught up trying to please the world that we forget who and what truly matters: Christ. "Whatever you do, work heartily, as for the Lord and not for men, knowing that from the Lord you will receive the inheritance as your reward. You are serving the Lord Christ" (Colossians 3:23-24).

I was available for everyone but myself, running myself ragged to be present, showing up for every event, yet didn't show up for myself, let alone make time to spend time with God. We often build selfish ways that make us feel better about ourselves or are too focused on heightening our reputation with others as a desire to be accepted. **The desire to be accepted in this world is the greatest originator of dishonor**. We look to please the social media world for likes to build our happiness. But we are not the likes and comments of social media. We are who God says we are, and just because someone likes or comments on every post does not mean you are truly liked or accepted. God already accepts us, and we forget that He is always present for us. So, whose approval are we really trying to win?

Galatians 1:10 reminds us: "Am I now trying to win the approval of human beings, or of God? Or am I trying to please people? If I were still trying to please people, I would not be a servant of Christ."

Can you answer those questions from Galatians?

Am I trying to win the approval of human beings or of God?

Am I trying to people-please?

Seeking the approval of others can lead you away from the direction that God may be trying to lead you. It says in His Word that if we are still trying to please people, we would not be servants of Christ. I would rather be a servant of Christ and present for whoever He sees fit for my life. Ask God to remove any person in your life that doesn't help you grow, give you Godly counsel instead of gossip, tell you right and wrong, and love you from non-judgmental places. Because **no one can judge you but God!**

Reflection

What wisdom did you gain from today's devotional?

_____

_____

_____

_____

_____

_____

_____

_____

_____

_____

_____

_____

_____

_____

_____

_____

_____

_____

Day 17

Relationship with God

Spending time with God is the key to our strength. **Time spent alone with God is never wasted.** It's building a relationship with Him so that you have guidance daily. It's that just-between-us intimate relationship with God, and it comes from the heart. The definition of relationship speaks to a connection. When we encounter people, we build friendships based on similar interests, and the support through ups and downs. When you encounter good friends, it becomes easier to deal with life's trials. But what if I told you that a relationship with God tops any connection in friendship or relationship? He wants to spend time with us for the rest of our lives, and though that may be the intention of many, that's one relationship you will never have to question. A relationship with God is the best relationship you can have and the greatest love you could ever receive. God wants a relationship with us. Revelation 3:20 states, "Behold I stand at the door and knock. If any man hears my voice and opens the door, I will come into him and will sup with him and he with me."

The key question is will you open the door with the right motives to build a relationship? How you come to God matters! "And he said to all, "If anyone would come after me, let him deny himself and take up his cross daily and follow me" (Luke 9:23).

Do you think your relationship with God is primarily in terms of what is in it for you or based on what you can do for Him? Luke 9:23 expresses coming after God, denying yourself, picking up His cross daily, and following Him. These directions could not be any clearer!

1. Come after God.

2. Deny yourself.

3. Pick up His cross daily.

4. Follow Him.

When we come after God, He receives us with open arms. There is no greater joy than being accepted, wanted, and loved by the Father. When we deny ourselves, our hearts are open and ready to receive all He has in store for us. Don't immediately think of tangible things like houses, cars, and money. I'm referring to intangible things we can't touch, like love, wisdom, favor, and joy. Picking up His cross daily means denying ourselves daily to be more like Him and letting go of any ways that could come between a relationship with God. It also means being humbly open to receive the truths of God's Word.

Are you willing to deny yourself, take up your cross, and follow Him?

Are you willing to follow Jesus if it means losing some of your closest friends or being alienated from family?

Are you willing?

A relationship with God is more important than just going to church and reading the Word. It's love, trust, and fellowship between you and the Father. It is getting up daily to bond with Him and talking to Him throughout your day. Sometimes we think that our conversations with Him must be perfect, but that's not the case. Just as you converse with your parents, family, and friends is the same way you can have a conversation with God about anything. He wants us to talk and spend time with Him daily. Even though He already knows what's on our minds, He still wants to hear from us no matter what. Doing so builds a steady relationship with God. **A relationship with God brings change. Change equals growth, and growth equals transformation.**

Reflection

There is no better relationship than with God. Once that relationship is in place, the right ones will fall in place. How important to you is a relationship with God?

_____

_____

_____

_____

_____

_____

_____

_____

_____

_____

_____

_____

_____

_____

_____

"The only thing necessary for the triumph of evil is for good men to do nothing."

(Edmund Burke)

Day 18

Learning How to Be Obedient

At one point in time, the word "obedient" did not quite roll off my tongue so easily. If I'm being honest, it wasn't in the forefront of my mind, either. Growing up, I was so used to doing what I wanted that the only thing I was partially obedient to was being in a relationship with someone. I was faithful to a lot of people, places, and things. However, my judgment in character led me to people that I shouldn't have been with and places I should not have visited. I was far from obedient. I was faithful to many things that were not conducive to my growth.

I can admit being obedient is not always easy because we want to do what we want, when and how we want to do it. We have the choice to go where we want to go, talk to whoever we want to talk to, take advice from anybody, build relationships with those we see fit, and make unhealthy choices. Sometimes our choices leave us lost or confused because we never consulted with God first in anything. That is not the workmanship of God. **Obedience is an act** and most definitely a choice to show our love to God. **We must trust God enough to live according to His ways**, trusting in Him and the direction He wants to take us. Through our obedience, we become planted in Him. And when we are planted in Him, nothing can deter us from that walk. "He is like a tree planted beside streams of water that bears its fruit in season and whose leaf does not wither. Whatever he does prospers" (Psalm 1:3).

God wants us to live our lives in obedience to His Word so that we can live out the Will He has for our lives. His Word is true and living and bigger than any word anyone could ever give us. There is power in His Word alone! There is peace when we surrender our ways and joy as a person of faith who not only walks but lives what they believe. Being planted means you are the tree that will always grow because you have sought God's ways. Beside the stream of water means that when there's little rain, you can draw from Him; His streams of water will always replenish you. Through your faithfulness and obedience, your tree will always bear fruit in the right seasons, and your leaves will not wither. Whatever you do will prosper because you have stayed connected to the vine of God and remained obedient.

I'm not saying that every day will be perfect, but I know that when I have fallen off, I immediately repented and asked for forgiveness. I did not repent to turn around and do it again because I knew He would forgive me. Instead, I repented because repentance is a part of being obedient. **A mistake repeated more than once is a decision.** Obedience is a responsibility I don't take lightly. Because we are living sacrifices of Christ, the righteousness of God is manifested through us because of our obedience. As I've grown, I've found joy in being obedient. God's reward for acts of obedience is greater than any gift I could ever give to myself. The walk with our Father is greater than any walk we can attempt on our own. I want the life that God desires for me, and so should you! *Try Jesus!*

Reflection

How will you apply obedience to your life?

_____

_____

_____

_____

_____

_____

_____

_____

What will you do differently?

_____

_____

_____

_____

_____

_____

_____

_____

Day 19

Persistence

When difficulty hits in life, sometimes it's easier to give up than to keep going. You may often think that overcoming what you are facing is not possible. Persistence is to continue firmly and steadily despite difficulties. But as we face difficulty, the real solution is how we react and handle our situations. Isaiah 41:10 states, "Fear not for I am with you, be not dismayed for I am your God. I will strengthen you; I will help you; I will uphold you with my righteous right hand."

The devil will try and bring opposition daily if you let him. But do you give up when tough obstacles are in front of you, or do you push through no matter what? Pushing through and not giving up would be the best choice, but I can admit that it's easier said than done. I remember when I laid in what I thought was defeat, and as I looked in the mirror, I thought less of myself. The real defeat was doubting myself and putting myself down. The real defeat was allowing depression to enter and stay. The real defeat was allowing others to tell me who I was and what I could not do when God said I was more than a conqueror. Persistence means to continue and not stop even when you feel like you can't make it. You are still here, which means another chance to keep going. I am here to tell you that by pushing through those obstacles, you're going to come out saying, "I'm glad I didn't give up." It's the best feeling in the world, seeing yourself come out of what you thought wasn't possible. That's when we know it's all God. Amid difficulties, we fail to realize that we should not attempt to do things in our strength but with God's strength. "I can do all things through Christ who strengthens me" (Philippians 4:13).

"Through Christ who strengthens me" is built on the internal, not external. Because of His strength, we can do anything. In the tough times, pushing through those obstacles with God's strength is a great honor. When you feel like giving up, tell God you need His strength to make it through, and He will strengthen and sustain you. Those moments are tests of faith. Believe, even when you feel it's not working. Be persistent in the mind. You've survived it all. God is our strong tower!

Reflection

Persistence means to continue and not give up. Anything is possible. Always finish what you start, asking God for the Finisher's anointing! What have you put down that you know you need to finish?

_____

_____

_____

_____

_____

_____

_____

_____

_____

_____

_____

_____

_____

_____

_____

_____

_____

_____

Day 20

When God Says No

Who likes the word no? I know I don't, but of course, we think life would be great if we could always get our way. What if God always gave us what we wanted? I've asked God for a few things in life that I was not quite prepared to receive. I had to learn the hard way that "no" is not always denial. It means that what you are asking for is not needed, won't grow you spiritually, or serve you well. Several times in my life, I fought for things and people, only to end up with my feelings crushed or picking up my heart off the ground, and it wasn't in one piece either. I took myself through the tough battles and drawn-out journeys because I didn't listen and wanted what I thought was good for me. I had to learn that God comes in His timing and not mine and that His thoughts and needs for me are always better.

I thought back to when I was younger, and my mother told me I could not do something, and I turned right around and did it anyway. It never failed to come back around and bite me. Sometimes, God says no because what we want is not good for us. Often, we want to learn and figure things out on our own, but some of those moments are not always necessary to learn the hard way. Sometimes, no is to protect both parties. Well, God says no, just like our parents, and it's in our best interest to listen to Him as well. When God says no and we don't listen, the consequences are like the consequences of our parents. If our parents said no, they more than likely knew we were not prepared for what comes with what we're asking, that it could be dangerous, or they've already experienced the area we want to explore. If God says no, the same applies. He is protecting us from ourselves and the hurt and pain that could result from diving into areas not fit for our lives. Patience is very important. In most cases, if I had been patient, I could have received what I had been asking for, if not greater, but in His timing.

When we do things in our timing, we're prematurely hopping into areas of life we are not fully prepared to encounter. Sometimes, we stretch the Word of God to make it say what we want it to say, convincing ourselves that our decisions and actions are okay. But God's plans are to prosper us, and His plans will never harm us. In fact, His plans give us hope and a future (Jeremiah 29:11). When we do what we want and ignore what God said, we end up forcing our will. You will remember the consequences to not go back down the same path again. Even though God's no may hurt, our trials are never a punishment. They help us grow and blossom by learning from our mistakes. There is purpose in our trials.

1 Peter 1:6-7 states:

So be truly glad. There is wonderful joy ahead, even though you must endure many trials for a little while. These trials will show that your faith is genuine. It is being tested as fire tests and purifies gold though your faith is far more precious than mere gold. So, when your faith remains strong through many trials, it will bring you much praise and glory and honor on the day when Jesus Christ is revealed to the whole world.

Believing that God is faithful and good means trusting Him in all situations, even when He says no. That means trusting Him while going through trials and tribulations, not just when things are good. We trust Him because there is a wonderful journey ahead. We must remember who has the final say, which is not us. We are to obey Christ. He will give us what's good for us when the time is right. Being patient is the key.

Reflection

Patience is a virtue. Without patience, it is impossible to serve God. We will face temptation and many challenges, but we must remain focused on our service to God.

What are you patiently waiting on God to do?

How are you waiting on God? In anger or joy? Impatiently or patiently? Fearful or trusting God?

Day 21

Godly Community

Community is God's desire for us!

Have you ever heard anyone say, "It takes a village"? Growing up, my mom's best friends were considered my aunts. They helped give out all the extra hugs and love and were present for life events. We were considered a team, a village, and they filled in the gaps when needed. As Christians, we want Godly friends and a genuine community. God never intended for us to be in this world alone. A Godly community shares a common life in Christ, committing ourselves to a life together as the true people of God. Being loved and appreciated by others is a natural desire that all of us want in life. But a Godly community is not always easy to come by because we are all on different walks in life. Our walks can carry us to different places and different stages in our faith journey. But Galatians 6:2 says, "and to bear their burdens alongside them." We are to be here for one another and gracefully bear each other's burdens, helping each other overcome. Not be judgmental, manipulative, self-centered, controlling, jealous, or make others feel bad about themselves. We are to experience life with people that we can laugh, cry with, and overcome pain with, but the true purpose of a Godly community is to experience the walk and love of God together.

On this walk, we will experience the love of God through each other. Can you imagine a life free of drama, no one judging you for your mistakes, people that pray with you and love you from a place with pure intentions? This is God's purpose for community, for Christians that love the Lord and know He died on the cross for us. If your community of friends does not look this, it's time to re-evaluate your circle.

Today, love from a pure place. Ask God to purify your heart and mind. Being a Godly friend is strengthening the faith of our friends and family with every opportunity and with the strength, faith, and love of God that He has given you. **We are Christ Representers!**

Reflections

The remnant remains! What opportunities will you take to build a Godly community?

_____

_____

_____

_____

_____

_____

_____

How are you a Christ Representer?

_____

_____

_____

_____

_____

_____

_____

_____

HEALING

Day 22

How to Deal with Your Heart

How to deal with matters of the heart is important. And if you're reading this today, it means that your heart is still beating. **Thank You, Jesus!**

Some of us have healthy hearts full of love, peace, and joy. Others have unhealthy hearts that need medication to function daily, hearts that have been broken, torn, and scared, or hearts that hold grudges and unforgiveness. What kind of heart do you hold today?

Of course, everyone wants a healthy heart, but let's be honest, not everyone's heart is healthy. And that's because the things we house in our hearts cause unhealthy functions. We can house so much in our hearts that bleed into natural action. Your actions show where your heart stands by how you treat God, yourself, and others. I can name a few things that caused me to house an unhealthy heart, one being the unforgiveness I held in my heart for my mother because she let her drug addiction carry her away from being present. The buildup of anger, hurt, and unforgiveness in my heart blocked me from loving her where she was at. Instead, I judged her with a stony heart. I hardened my heart toward my mother with no sympathy for someone who needed the same love I needed. Secondly, I've housed a heart that has been broken because I entrusted the wrong individuals with my heart. I stepped into relationships that were not meant to handle my heart, and they either handled it the best way they knew how or didn't care at all. Lastly, I've housed a heart that has been shattered from the death of loved ones, not knowing if the pieces of my heart could ever be restored. I'm here to tell you that all the matters of the heart can be treated with the love of God. And because He is the only true Healer of an unhealthy heart, He is the only one who can mend our broken, torn, and bruised hearts. Because our hearts truly belong to Him, we can house the heart of God today. Deuteronomy 6:5 states, "Love the Lord your God with all your heart, with all your soul and with all your strength." Would you rather have a stony heart or a heart that will love and obey our God?

Ezekiel 36:26 says, "A new heart also will I give you, and a new spirit will I put within you: and I will take away the stony heart out of your flesh, and I will give you a heart of flesh." Today think about the condition of your heart. Tell God everything that is on your heart, good or bad. It doesn't matter; He just wants to hear it from you. Ask Him to remove any fear, doubt, resentment, or hurt, anger, or jealousy and to fill your heart with love, peace, and joy!

Reflection

What's on your heart today?

_____

_____

_____

_____

_____

_____

_____

_____

_____

_____

_____

_____

_____

_____

_____

_____

_____

_____

_____

_____

_____

_____

Day 23

Forming Habits

They say it takes 21 days to break or form a habit. I often wondered who came up with that number. I was taught that consistency was key and what we repeatedly do shows our true character. Truthfully, habits are tough to break when you have been conditioned to certain ways. It's hard to let go of ways we've been customized to, and sometimes we don't want to let go. But the point is to form and build healthy habits, and with consistency, things will become easier, which is why consistency is key. I've learned that when we continuously put things off as a tomorrow task, it only takes a few times to fall off and back into old cycles. So, if excellence is key, let's make it a habit to strive for excellence rather than just talking about it. We must follow through with repetition because **habit is overcome by habit**. Change does not happen overnight, and it isn't always easy. But with time and effort, almost any habit can be reshaped. God wants us to build good habits pertaining to ourselves and Him included, such as spending time with Him and developing or building a prayer life. Being persistent in forming Godly habits and not giving up when you want to step back into old habits is pertinent. If you believe you can change, make it a habit, and the change becomes real. Place yourself in a Godly community that will help you push through your habits, people with the same perspective in life and living for God. Remember, motivation is what gets you started, but habit is what keeps you going.

1 Timothy 4:7-10 reminds us:

Have nothing to do with irreverent, silly myths. Rather train yourself for godliness; for while bodily training is of some value, godliness is of value in every way, as it holds promise for the present life and also for the life to come. The saying is trustworthy and deserving of full acceptance. For to this end, we toil and strive because we have our hope set on the living God, who is the Savior of all people, especially of those who believe.

If habit is what keeps you going, what habits are you building? I'm not talking about habits in the natural; I'm speaking of habits of holiness. As the Scripture says that bodily training is of some value, **Godliness is of value in every way**. Godliness flows in every area of your life, and it also holds the promise for the present life of what you're living in now and what's to come. This spiritual exercise has unlimited value. It brings blessings for now and eternity. With our hopes set on the living God, we can attain the promise of abundant life and blessings. So, watch the kind of habits you form and make sure they will lead you to God.

Reflections

What habits are you exercising today? List your good habits and bad habits.

_____

_____

_____

_____

_____

_____

_____

_____

_____

What changes do you need to make?

_____

_____

_____

_____

_____

_____

_____

_____

_____

Day 24

Making Better Choices

Making the right choices can be hard. We can be led by many different things that could cause us to make the wrong decisions. Without a plan and discipline, making better choices can be hard. Have you ever heard the saying, "When you know better, you do better"? Because when you know better, the expectation is that you do better, but it does not always pan out that way. You have a choice to do right or wrong. As we grow, there is a responsibility that falls on us to know the difference.

When faced with two or more possibilities, we have the right to say yes or no. In all life's decisions, the most important choice is choosing who you live for. You have a choice to serve God our Father or serve Satan, the father of all lies. **There is no in-between**. The enemy can't stop what God has for you, but our choices can hinder you, including hindering your growth. Choosing who you serve will help you to make better choices. We cannot just think about ourselves when making decisions because God should be front and center in every decision we make—keeping in mind that my actions may not only affect me but could affect those I love as well. Here is a question to think about: Do you love God and yourself enough to let go of the things that drain you and pull you away from God?

If the answer is no, He won't be able to fully move in your life or heart because you won't have room to receive. You must love yourself enough to live in the freedom of not being held down by people, places, and things that no longer serve where you are going or letting the enemy lead you down paths of destruction. You must understand that God wants to take you places, and some people are not meant to go because they are not headed where you are. **God is the only one who can take you where He wants you to be**. You must use the wisdom of learning from your mistakes to excel in life.

Choosing to live a righteous life is a surrender to the Holy Spirit, and it's the best choice to make. This means that every good work in your life is an act of Christ in you (2 Timothy 3:17). Making the right choices has not always been easy, and I've had my fair share of consequences for my disobedience. I have made poor choices in friendships and relationships, in school, and pertaining to myself. In all my poor choices, I did not consult with God. As I have lived and learned, I can say today that thinking about God first before making any choice makes all the difference. Invite God in to help you with your decision-making. Learn to ask Him the simplest things: should I take this phone call, should I go to this party, or what should I wear? You may think that's unnecessary, but I soon realized how much I left God out of my everyday life. Every day won't be easy street, and He didn't promise us perfection, but with your consistency, He will be honored to help you flow in His Will every day of your life. Here is a verse to keep with you: "Let the wise hear and increase in learning, and the one who understands obtain guidance" (Proverbs 1:5).

Remember, keep God first in all that you do!

Reflections

There is always room for improvement! In what areas of your life can you make better choices?

_____

_____

_____

_____

_____

_____

_____

_____

_____

_____

_____

_____

_____

_____

_____

_____

_____

Day 25

Unforgiveness

Forgiveness can be the hardest thing in life for many of us to handle. We can hold onto unforgiveness for years and even take it to the grave with us. But that's not the life that God intended for us to live, a life with hurt, pain, anger, and bitterness embedded in our hearts. I learned that forgiveness is not for the individual who hurt you. Instead, **forgiveness is for you**. Forgiveness is for your healing, and it opens space in your heart for God to show you how your heart is supposed to love, like His.

Forgiveness was by far the hardest task for me to do. I say this because I had a lot of forgiving to do. I had to forgive my parents for not being in my life as responsible parents. I had to forgive my grandmother for the verbal and physical abuse growing up. I had to forgive my molesters, friends I thought were friends, and myself for the things I had to do to survive. My list could go on and on. But I am here to let you know that forgiveness is possible. It's possible to forgive people and still love them as God calls us to, but you don't have to rebuild those relationships unless God leads you to do so.

Sometimes we wait around for an apology that we may never receive because we set expectations for others, and they don't even know that we've set those expectations for them. So, while we wait on an apology, the individual that caused the pain could be living life freely while we're holding onto hurt, anger, and unforgiveness.

What if you never receive an apology?

I was allowing waiting on an apology to hinder my growth. I became stagnant because I could not let go of the past. I could not let go of what was done to me or said to me. I became an angry woman. My unforgiveness poured into my relationships. I began to make other people pay for the actions of others, and they didn't deserve the backlash or my poor attitude when all they wanted to do was show me love. But I had no space in my heart to be loved properly. I held onto so much that my heart and mind were paying the price because I was too deep in my emotions to be led by the Holy Spirit.

Unwillingness to forgive is a choice. We have a choice to forgive. In this decision, you choose whether to hold a grudge against the individual who offended you, leaving no compassion to forgive. But did you know that unforgiveness is a sin?

Ephesians 4:31 states:

Get rid of all bitterness, rage, anger, harsh words, and slander as well as all types of evil behavior. Instead, be kind to each other, tenderhearted, forgiving one another just as God through Christ has forgiven you.

Unforgiveness can cause us to think or do wicked things. It could cause us to try and take matters into our own hands and become vengeful. Romans 12:19 states, "Do not take revenge, my dear friends, but leave room for God's wrath, for it is written: 'It is mine to avenge; I will repay,' says the Lord."

God has our backs! I remember seeing individuals I was holding grudges against continuously prosper in life, and I wondered why I was still in the same place. It was because I was the one walking around with the attitude and feeling like I could never forgive those that wronged me and that they owed me something. Sometimes, I had no intentions of forgiving them, but that is not a path we should travel.

What if as much as we didn't forgive others, God did not forgive us for the things that we do that are not pleasing to Him? Matthew 18:33 reminds us, "Shouldn't you have mercy on your fellow servants, just as I had mercy on you?"

Today, let's forgive! Let's have a conversation with God and ask Him to help our unforgiving hearts.

Reflections

Today, we are no longer waiting on apologies from others. We are surrendering these ways to God and freeing ourselves from any offense. Trust God when life gets tough!

Remember, forgiveness is for you and not them.

Let's Stay Connected!

 @CarlaChalk

 @CarlaChalk

 www.carlachalk.com

Made in the USA
Coppell, TX
16 December 2021

68890427R00069